W9-BAK-956

A Thousand Paths to Confidence

A Thousand Paths to
confidence

David Baird

MQP

Contents

Introduction

What is confidence? Where does it come from and how can you get some?

There isn't anybody, certainly that I know of, who does not wish to live in a confident world, to be a confident person, to have confidence in themselves and what they do, and to enjoy the confidence of others in them. Yet why is it that, for some of us, confidence is so elusive when others seem to be oozing with confidence and only ever appear to be doing well?

Most of us have some belief in our potential and abilities, and we have all been born with the equal possibility of success.

If only we could get to grips with confidence and bring it to the forefront of our lives and into all that we do…But to achieve this, we need to take our first confident leap, or small step for the faint-hearted, and gather momentum from there.

The more we can understand about the nature of confidence, the sooner we can dispel all the myths that may have been holding us back from becoming confident people. Confidence is not about thinking we are better than everyone else, but is an awareness of our attributes, and having the courage to acknowledge them and put them to use.

First Steps
to
Confidence

Every moment of our life is absolutely precious and is not to be wasted in self-doubt. The wish to be confident and to live life with confidence is the vital first step. If you are prepared to take it, congratulate yourself—you have begun your journey on the path to confidence.

Do you tend to stay in your comfort zone, fear failure, and avoid taking risks? Strive to become more outgoing and sure about yourself.

Make people feel they can instantly be comfortable with you.

Get to know what other people are thinking and feeling.

Improve your performance in any area of your life and when you do, move onto another one!

Do you tend to tailor your behavior to fit what other people think it should be?

Become the person you want to be.

It is possible to sway other people's minds without too much difficulty.

Start transforming the way people see you.

Convert each failure or part of a failure into a success.

We climb to heaven most often on the ruins of our cherished plans, finding our failures were successes.
Amos Bronson Alcott

Reach a level where you need never feel uncomfortable with strangers again.

Strangers are just friends I haven't met yet.

Will Rogers

Achieve a rapport with individuals and whole groups of people.

To associate with other like-minded people in small, purposeful groups is for the great majority of men and women a source of profound psychological satisfaction.

Aldous Huxley

Discover how, simply by changing the way you say things, you can improve not only your life but that of others.

The universe is change.

Marcus Aurelius

Abandon your old negative habits and help others to do likewise.

Habits change into character.

Ovid

Get the job you want even if you have to create it. Somebody somewhere wants and needs what you can and want to do.

Pleasure in the job puts perfection in the work.

Aristotle

Enjoy all your senses more fully than ever before. Go out and see the world. Really look at it and sample the pleasures of art, music, and architecture, and the diversity of human interaction.

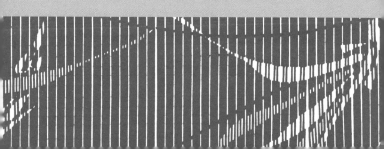

Each day I live in a glass
room unless I break it with
the thrusting of my senses
and pass through the
splintered walls to the
great landscape.

Mervyn Peake

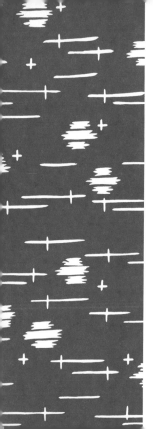

Create new family unity. Try to be forgiving and offer others the chance to be forgiving toward you.

Men's hearts ought not to be set against one another, but set with one another, and all against evil only.

Thomas Carlyle

Achieve your goals by controlling your words.

Eating words has never given me indigestion.

Winston Churchill

Get people to do what you want by utilizing their use of language, and their words.

You can stroke people with words.

F. Scott Fitzgerald

Dissipate all long-standing
rows and disagreements.

**We are not won by arguments that
we can analyze, but by tone and
temper; by the manner, which is the
man himself.**

Samuel Butler

Discover the questions that can change your life.

It's better to know some of the questions than all of the answers.

James Thurber

Get people to leave you alone when you want them to.

Selfishness is not living as one wishes to live; it is asking others to live as one wishes to live. And unselfishness is letting other people's lives alone, not interfering with them. Selfishness always aims at uniformity of type. Unselfishness recognizes infinite variety of type as a delightful thing, accepts it, acquiesces in it, enjoys it.

Oscar Wilde

Instead of avoiding people who are furious, try dealing with them.

Beware the fury of a patient man.

John Dryden

Get what you want by asking for advice.

Many receive advice, only the wise profit from it.

Publilius Syrus

Stop people from making you feel guilty.

When good people have a falling-out,
only one of them may be at fault at first;
but if the strife continues long, usually
both become guilty.

Thomas Fuller

Put the power of silence to work for you.

I often regret that I have spoken; never that I have been silent.

Publilius Syrus

Work on ways to get other people to make up their minds.

He who wants to persuade should put his trust not in the right argument, but in the right word. The power of sound has always been greater than the power of sense.

Joseph Conrad

Negotiate successfully. Learn the secrets of give and take.

Let us never negotiate out of fear but let us never fear to negotiate.

John F. Kennedy

Recognize and take advantage of the fact that life is filled with wonderful coincidences.

Any person can begin achieving things they believed were beyond their dreams, simply through the elimination of two little words from their vocabulary: "I" and "can't".

Become not only tolerated, but spellbinding!

We cannot always control our thoughts, but we can control our words, and repetition impresses the subconscious, and we are then master of the situation.

Florence Scovel Shinn

Recognize that we each have within us the potential to alter the belief patterns, of not only individuals, but immeasurable numbers of people.

I have with me two gods, Persuasion and Compulsion.

Themistocles

Become trustworthy and trusted.

**To be trusted
is a greater
compliment than
to be loved.**
  George MacDonald

Get your
boss on
your side.

Win arguments
as amicably
as possible.

Your real boss is the one who walks around under your hat.

Napoleon Hill

Sell yourself successfully and influence people.

Even though it is essential for us to acknowledge our successes, it is not good to brag—it is better to make the big celebration private and share the victory sensitively with those around you in a manner that can motivate them.

We are all salesmen every day of our lives. We are selling our ideas, our plans, our enthusiasms to those with whom we come in contact.

Charles M. Schwab

Never employ the wrong person again.

Never work for the wrong person again.

Treat employees like partners, and they act like partners.

Fred A. Allen

Choose a job you love, and you will never have to work a day in your life.

Confucius

Enjoy being the creator of your own life without boring others by becoming vain.

A self-made man?
Yes, and one who
worships his creator.
William Cowper

Stop people from being negative about
themselves and certainly about you.

One's eyes are what one is, one's mouth is what one becomes.

John Galsworthy

Understand how people think—often one can tell by just looking into their eyes.

Control the secret messages your unconscious is capable of giving away to others. Don't always let the outward signs betray your inner thoughts.

To know that one has a secret is to know half the secret itself.

Henry Ward Beecher

Let anger glide past you like water off a duck's back.

People deal too much with the negative, with what is wrong. Why not try and see positive things, to just touch those things and make them bloom?
Thich Nhat Hanh

When angry, count to four; when very angry, swear.

Mark Twain

Enjoy all the benefits of instant bonding. Even two total strangers can find common ground.

Confidence is the bond of friendship.

Publilius Syrus

Learn to smile with your eyes.

The eyes are not responsible when the mind does the seeing.

Publilius Syrus

Asking for advice from colleagues
is not a sign of lack of confidence
—it shows that you respect them
and that you have taken their
viewpoints into consideration
before making difficult decisions.

Do you spend most of your time working hard to cover up mistakes and praying that nobody notices before you've had time to fix them? Admit your mistakes and vow to learn from them.

Low self-confidence can be self-destructive, and it tends to manifest itself as negativity.

Self-confident people are generally more positive—they believe in themselves, their abilities, and the wonders of living life to the full.

Do what you believe to be right, even if others mock or criticize you for it.

Become willing to take risks and go the extra mile to achieve better things.

Meditation can do away with despair and make you feel supported by a new confidence, which is endowed with possibility and the power to act.

Which are you:
the person waiting
for others to
congratulate them
on their
accomplishments,
or the person
who busies
themself extolling
their own
virtues as often as
possible to
as many people
as possible?

Do you dismiss compliments off-handedly? Accept them graciously. It means that others have noticed your efforts and you are entitled to feel pleased with yourself.

Try not to feel desperate when things don't go as planned.

View each challenge as an opportunity to grow and learn.

The confident person does not dwell on negative events.

Put a positive spin onto any negative things that happen—focus on what you have learned as an individual or as a team from the experience.

'Tis said, best men are moulded of their faults.

William Shakespeare

Some of your griefs you have cured,
And the sharpest you still have survived;
But what torments of pain you endured
From evils that never arrived!

Old French saying

**When you believe in
yourself and dream big,
anything is possible.**

Insist on yourself; never imitate.
Your own gift you can present every
moment with the cumulative force of a
whole life's cultivation; but of the adopted
talent of another, you have only an
extemporaneous half possession.

Ralph Waldo Emerson

Believe in a hope that a new hope is dawning…
Believe that your dreams will come true…
Believe in the promise of brighter tomorrows…
Begin by believing in you.

Confidence gives us a whole new outlook;
a whole new set of attitudes to life.
It illuminates everything around us.
Suddenly there are opportunities everywhere.

They've got us surrounded again, the poor bastards.

Creighton Abrams

Confidence…thrives on honesty, on honor, on the sacredness of obligations, on faithful protection, and on unselfish performance. Without them it cannot live.

Franklin D. Roosevelt

The person who makes a success of living is the one who sees his goal steadily and aims for it unswervingly. That is dedication.

Cecil B. DeMille

Nobody climbs mountains for scientific reasons. Science is used to raise money for the expeditions, but you really climb for the hell of it.

Sir Edmund Hillary

If I have the belief that I can do it, I shall surely acquire the capacity to do it even if I may not have it at the beginning.

Mahatma Gandhi

Never bend your head. Always hold it high. Look the world straight in the face.

Helen Keller

An optimist is a person who sees a green light everywhere; while a pessimist sees only the red stop light. The truly wise person is color-blind.

Dr. Albert Schweitzer

Take a chance! All life is a chance. The man who goes the furthest is generally the one who is willing to do and dare. The "sure thing" boat never gets far from shore.

Dale Carnegie

Looking positive not only gives the impression of confidence, but it will make you feel better about yourself.

He only is a well-made man who has a good determination. And the end of culture is not to destroy this—God forbid! —but to train away all impediment and mixture and leave nothing but pure power.

Ralph Waldo Emerson

No man is quite sane; each has a vein of folly in his composition, a slight determination of blood to the head, to make sure of holding him hard to some one point which nature has taken to heart.

Ralph Waldo Emerson

Thou must be like a promontory of the sea, against which though the waves beat continually, yet it both itself stands, and about it are those swelling waves stilled and quieted.

Marcus Aurelius

Everyone who has tried has failed at something and to most it didn't matter and they tried again.

A lotta cats copy the *Mona Lisa*, but people still line up to see the original.

Louis Armstrong

Whoever deliberately attempts to insure confidentiality with another person is usually in doubt as to whether he inspires that person's confidence in him. One who is sure that he inspires confidence attaches little importance to confidentiality.

Friedrich Nietzsche

Nothing in the world can take the place of
Persistence.
Talent will not; nothing is more common
than unsuccessful men with talent.
Genius will not; unrewarded genius is
almost a proverb.
Education will not; the world is full of
educated derelicts.
Persistence and Determination alone
are omnipotent.
The slogan "Press On" has solved and
will always solve the problems of the
human race.

Calvin Coolidge

People who give us their full confidence believe that they have thereby earned a right to ours. This is a fallacy; one does not acquire rights through gifts.

Friedrich Nietzsche

No man ever quite believes in any other man. One may believe in an idea absolutely, but not in a man. In the highest confidence there is always a flavor of doubt—a feeling, half instinctive and half logical, that, after all, the scoundrel may have something up his sleeve.

Henry Lewis Mencken

Write a list of every little accomplishment, achievement, skill, or talent to remind you of what you have going for you.

Life is an art. It is the art of selecting that for which you are apt: architecture or poetry; politics or sport. All are achievable when we know who we are.

Confidence does not remove the capacity for us to be surprised. There will always be that look on the face of all who are present at the birth of a child, on the face of the doctor who manages to mend a patient, on the face of the athlete who wins the race…And on our own face when we look in the mirror and say, "I did it!"

Sincerity is an openness of heart which we unfortunately find in very few people. Instead we are faced with a form of artful dissimulation designed to win our confidence.

The Nature
of the Thing

Confidence is a formidable energy.

We all have the capacity to pretend to be confident; and if we have that, we also have what it takes to actually be confident.

We are born with natural confidence within us: why otherwise would we have taken our first breath, our first steps, or said our first words? The same confidence that gave us life hasn't left us, but it can become clouded over by doubt.

Be confident in what you leave behind after your time on this Earth. Nothing can erase the good deeds you have done, be it fire, wind, birth, or death.

Insincere and evil friends are to be feared more than beasts; beasts may wound your body, but people can wound your mind and heart.

Be confident that when the mind becomes pure then our surroundings will also become pure.

In your quest for self-confidence it is better to conquer yourself than to win a thousand other battles— then the victory is yours alone. The confidence you gain can never be taken from you by anyone or anything.

Have confidence in friends who point out your mistakes and imperfections—they are to be cherished and respected for they have the map to your hidden treasure.

Profit and respect are like stones on the path to confidence and should be brushed aside before they trip you up.

If you can find it within you to repent your wrongdoings, they will disappear and life can move forward.

Confident people do not believe in anything simply because they have heard it.

As irrigators confidently lead water where they want, as archers confidently make their arrows straight, as carpenters confidently carve wood, so the wise confidently shape their minds.

Value every moment of your life, and concentrate on what must be done in the present moment. Do not dwell in the past; do not dwell in the future: concentrate the mind on the present moment and find confidence in that moment.

The world is so filled with people busy trying to be different. Instead of joining them, be good and do good. That is different enough.

One does evil enough when one does nothing good.

Respect each other: refrain from disputes; forget your differences; when it comes to reconciliation, remember water and oil repel each other.

Believe nothing, no matter where you read it, or who said it, unless it agrees with your own reason and your own common sense.

Don't blame your enemies. It is one's own mind that lures one away from confidence.

It is a common misconception that some people are born leaders: they're not. Leaders are made; it takes hard work to develop the confidence to lead others.

People more often than not are harder on themselves than they are on others. How often have you heard someone say: "I'm so useless" or "I'm ugly" or "I'm too fat"? Chances are you've said something similar about yourself.

Confidence provides those who possess it with a resolute determination, the will to succeed.

Approach every burdensome task with enthusiasm, for nothing matches the surge of self-confidence that comes from accomplishing it.

Our emotions are fickle and are determined mainly by how we perceive and interpret what is going on around us. Recognize this and you can be confident that you will be able to find something positive in any situation.

If we can convince ourselves that there is no reason not to be confident, our emotions, thoughts, behavior and ideas will soon manifest in outer confidence.

Confidence is as much about knowing what we can't do as what we can do— it is about understanding and coming to terms with our capabilities.

The mind is like a parachute. If it is packed badly it may not open fully and cause a fall to the ground. But if time, concentration, and effort are invested in packing it, it will ensure a safe and invigorating descent.

Suddenly you will find yourself wondering why you managed to remain focused on your purpose without becoming stressed out. It is because you are confident!

Ask yourself whether you have what it takes to be assertive when it is appropriate to be so.

Self-confidence is what gives us true integrity. Integrity allows us to live our lives according to a set of values, acting and behaving in a manner considered right not only by us but also those around us.

Never place all your trust
in people who boast they are
"as honest as the day is long."
If they haven't got the
confidence to meet
you at night...

Look in the mirror and say aloud: "I have the confidence to go after my dreams".

A man can do all things if he but wills them.

Each time we face our fears head-on we gain strength and courage, and increase our confidence.

Life is like a wrestling match.
You struggle to stay on top of
events: if you let up, they will
surely be on top of you.

**Do you have a strong will?
Or a strong won't!**

Confidence is the feeling you have
even before you understand a situation.

Have confidence in yourself; take action; embrace life.

Our lives tend to move in the direction of our expectations, and the more determined and confident we become, the happier our lives are inclined to be.

Age and experience teach us to recognize and envy those with young hearts and self-confidence.

The confidence acquired with age is not usually matched by a corresponding open-mindedness to new ideas—much to the frustration of the young.

There is nothing to be gained from trying to iron out your neighbor's follies if you can't iron out your own with confidence.

Place more importance on what you can do than what you cannot.

Do you want to know what confidence is really all about?
It is about having the guts to treat ourselves better than we usually do.

Confident people are tactful.

Unfortunately we are compelled to share this world with people who feel it their duty to make others feel ashamed simply for being who they are. Take pride in yourself and these destructive forces cannot touch you.

Difficult people can challenge your self-belief. The moment you realize that their behavior boils down to a lack of self-esteem, you can relax in the confidence that your own is intact.

Stop thinking,
"What will
they think?"

Be assertive, yet considerate
of the feelings of others.

A confident speaker knows it is better to speak the truth simply than to be long-winded and divisive.

Keep managing your mind: stay on top of your positive thinking; keep enjoying and celebrating success; and keep those mental images confident and strong.

**Give yourself
good reasons
to trust yourself
more and more
every day.**

Be respectful of other
people's anxieties
when striving to bring
change about.
Change may inspire
you but terrify those
the changes will affect.

Winning breeds confidence, but confidence breeds winning.

In order to develop confidence in your ability to perform well, you must first lay the right foundation—the cornerstone of which is honesty.

Shake off your burdensome past! Grab back control of your life and make it happen.

Confident people recognize that one's weaker human inclinations toward vice are fueled by the company one chooses to keep, and so prefer to seek out the companionship of good people.

Save your applause for that generous and lofty spirit which inspires others with unbounded confidence, and opens their minds to the possibility that each day of battle is also a day of victory.

Self-confidence is often the result of a successfully survived risk.

Happiness is knowing confidently that the necessities of life will come to you without fear or severe strain.

Being confident is about knowing who you are: what it is you stand for; what it is that's important for you to be, do, and have in life.

Keep yourself grounded—it is a temptation to get over-confident and too cocky for your own good; then you suddenly find you have gone too near the edge of the cliff and go tumbling down. Catch yourself while you still can!

Dress confidently, but to be one of the team, not the focus of the team.

Confident people are people who believe in themselves; people who believe in themselves take charge of their actions.

Learn to be as pleasantly assertive as it is possible to be in any situation, but always state your point of view clearly without backing down.

Being confident is a feeling of certainty, self-belief, and freedom from doubt.

Toast your achievements with a glass of bubbly. But most importantly, give yourself a firm pat on the back.

Beware: weakness of attitude becomes weakness of character.

Make friends—you can confidently count on the fact that even with a single enemy in your life, you will meet him everywhere.

We are new every day, or at least have the potential to be.

Confident people tend to live up to their own expectations and beyond the expectations of those around them.

One needn't be disagreeable in order to disagree.

We are all human and touching is natural—it need not be regarded as a sexual approach. A simple hug from a colleague, friend, or partner can give you both an immense confidence boost.

Be confident in the company of true friends. With them we are easily great.

Each friend we have confirms there is some virtue in us that attracted them to us.

Yesterday is but a dream and
tomorrow is only a vision.
Live each and every day
with passion.

**People can only be happy
when they become
confident in the knowledge
that the sole object of
life is happiness.**

Start where you are.

When you can say to yourself with total conviction, "I can alter my life by altering the attitude of my mind, " you have started on the path to confidence.

**You must
first finish
in order to
finish first.**

Learn to respond to
people and situations
instead of reacting
to everything.
Reaction is
mostly perceived
as negativity.

Repeat this before
doing anything:
"If it is to be,
it is up to me."

Tell yourself: "I am a confident
individual and at last I feel
happy to put myself first."

By capacity-building, we reach levels of sustainable self-confidence and this frees us to confidently articulate our opinions and enter constructive debates.

With confidence, you win even before you start.

To gain the confidence of those around you, show them that you are flexible toward people and circumstances, and are not afraid of new things.

Confidence is about give and take. You must prove you are able to give genuine praise and to accept constructive criticism.

Decide exactly what you want to accomplish, then determine what personal physical/mental/time cost you are prepared to bear.

There is no miracle involved in confidence. It is personal application and perseverance prompted by a determined spirit.

The key to success is self-confidence. The key to that is preparation. Constant and determined effort breaks down all resistance and sweeps away all obstacles.

See first that the design is wise and just; that ascertained, pursue it resolutely.

William Shakespeare

Never repeat to anyone anything you do not have the confidence to sign your name to.

Walt Disney is alleged to have inspired his company to run on four Cs: curiosity, confidence, courage, consistency. And he saw confidence as the greatest of these.

Ask any coach, boss, employer, or leader what the very worst thing is that could happen to an individual or a player; a team or a business; an army or a nation; and they will tell you it is their loss of confidence.

A confidence game or trick is a swindle in which the victim is defrauded after his or her confidence has been won.

Self-esteem is about feeling good about ourselves—that we can feel secure in our ability to be competent and effective.

With confidence and determination you can do what you have to do and, more often than not, you will discover that you can do it even better than you think you can.

We all are all born and we all die. Somewhere in between there is a life that is yours to live.

Always seek to be as objective as you possibly can by seeking out and weighing up all the evidence that supports and goes against your thinking.

Feel optimistic and motivated to take the easy steps to a new and confident you.

Say to yourself: "I am a confident individual and I stand out from the crowd."

One may not reach the dawn save by the path of the night.

Confidence neither has trouble itself nor does it cause trouble for anyone else; it does not experience feelings of anger or indebtedness, for such feelings signify lack of confidence.

Pleasure reaches its maximum limit at the removal of all sources of anxiety.

One can walk throughout the dark night confident that in time and with patience one will arrive at the light of a new day.

She lacks confidence,
she craves admiration insatiably.
She lives on the reflections of
herself in the eyes of others.
She does not care to be herself.

Anaïs Nin

Confidence itself is not a sign
of truthfulness; just as a lack
of confidence does not make
a person false.

One can always have confidence in the fact that in union there is strength.

Confidence gives us patience. That alone is vital. With it anything is achievable over time.

Confidence only points the way.
You must set out on the journey
on your own.

**To learn to stay afloat
one must first have the
confidence to jump in.**

The greatest form of
confidence is knowing
how to be oneself.

A pessimist is one who makes difficulties of his opportunities and an optimist is one who makes opportunities of his difficulties.

Many take only their needs into consideration, rarely their abilities, and this is where their confidence awaits them.

You can only when you believe you can.

When one is not confident of living wisely, despite living honorably and justly, it is impossible to live a pleasant life.

If you carry with you through life the confidence of your inner freedom, you will never be the captive of anyone else.

Bind yourself to truth and live up to what you have.

People do not attract that which they want, but that which they are—and are just about as happy as they make up their minds to be.

Why fear life? It is a person's reluctance to believe that life is worth living that closes the gate to creating the fact.

Shake off your obstinate opinions. They will only hold you in chains with no hope of emancipation until you do so.

It doesn't matter how slow progress is—it, and those who are making it, should be encouraged.

If you want to be remembered by people for their entire lifetime, don't flatter or criticize them: encourage them instead.

Everybody is capable of something. It is down to each of us to put all our excuses aside and begin to discover what it is we can be confident of doing.

Confidence is less about
having the will to believe,
and more about having the
compelling desire to find out.

**Confidence is about having
spirit—the spirit to win,
to excel, and to endure—
it is more to do with these
than what one achieves
with them.**

Stop looking for your purpose.
You are your purpose, so be it!

Know yourself and you will have
what is necessary to overcome
all obstacles and win all battles.

No one is in control of your
confidence but you;
only you have the power
to change yourself
and your life.

If a person goes to his job with a firm determination to give of himself the best of which he is capable, that job—no matter what it is—takes on dignity and importance.

Confidence demands a fundamental change in our attitude toward life. Begin by asking yourself what life expects from you.

With even the fairest, most balanced odds and conditions, men still vacillate, unsure, locked firmly to the spot, afraid to move, while the confident remain immovably centered as they leap in with both feet.

Confidence is not about how much money you have; it is not about not being scared. It is about self-discipline and self-knowledge.

To become confident, one must learn to discount the negative and never ignore the positive.

Part of being confident is acting confidently. One must learn how to win gracefully and never to run away when one doesn't win.

The happiest people are those who enjoy a life with nothing to fear from those who surround them. These people live among one another most agreeably, having the firmest grounds for confidence in one another.

Only those who dare to fail greatly can ever achieve greatly.

Robert F. Kennedy

The
Foundation
is Integrity

**The foundation of confidence
is integrity. Talent is important
but is always dwarfed by integrity.**

Confidence consists in not
being subdued by your means.

Vigor is contagious! Whatever
makes us either think or feel
strongly adds to our power
and enlarges our field of action.

Why is it so difficult to be truly confident? Perhaps it is because even though we hunger for approval, we live in constant dread of condemnation.

Words have the power to destroy and heal. When words are both true and kind, you can be confident that they are able to change our world for the better.

To think is easy.

To act is difficult.

To act as one thinks: that is the most difficult.

On life's path, faith is our
nourishment. We take shelter
in our good deeds. Our way is
lit by wisdom and the confidence
we discover is our protection
from all that may harm us.

Just as one would never assume a dog to be good because it is good at barking, the same goes for mankind. No matter how good a talker someone is they must still have real goodness within them if they are to earn the confidence of those around them.

To him who is determined it remains only to act.

It never hurt anyone's self-confidence to have a mentor: someone you can respect who is positive and can encourage you.

Confident people do not believe in anything simply because it is spoken and rumored by many.

Consider a welltended garden where all the elements live confidently in harmony side by side, weathering the storms, sharing the sunlight. The same should be true of families and friendships.

On the long journey of human life, confidence is the best companion we could possibly ask for—with it everything we need for the journey is within our reach.

He is able who thinks he is able.

The peace and contentment that confidence brings comes from within. Do not waste your life seeking it without.

Doubt and jealousy are poisons that destroy friendships. When confidence is shattered, so too are relationships.

It's the mark of greatness for any person to be confident in tough situations.

Man needs a rule for his will, and is confident enough to invent one where one is not given him.

The whole secret of confident existence is to have no fear. Never live in fear of what may become of you, and try to become dependent upon no one other than yourself. Only the moment you reject such external fears and dependencies are you freed.

Kindness in giving creates love, but kindness in words creates confidence.

One should never allow one's confidence to be dashed by the insecurities or behavior of others—the world is full of bullies who are confident of getting away with it. Don't let them.

Nothing builds self-esteem and self-confidence like accomplishment.

Practice contentment. There is great comfort and confidence to be gained from it.

Many humans tend to base their opinions on a thought process that is "all or nothing." We all have our good and our bad points. If you encounter someone at a bad moment it doesn't mean that they are wholly bad.

Confidence is like a dance. You start with one step, then another and another.

Since you cannot tame the minds of others until you have tamed your own, begin there.

Those who stand for nothing fall for anything.

Alexander Hamilton

If you want to get somewhere, doesn't it make sense to plan ahead how to get there? This applies to life as much as to a car journey. It is also a great confidence boost to know how to change a tire or to have membership of an auto club before venturing forth!

I'd rather have a positive something than a negative nothing.

The difference between the confident person and the person with no confidence might be the difference between perceiving yourself as being temporarily broke and believing yourself to be helplessly poor.

Confidence does not exist only for an elite few. It is not a great secret ability that some have and others don't have. We all carry everything we need to be confident within us, and confidence will begin to manifest itself the very instant that you start to attach value to yourself, your thoughts, your ideas, and your methods.

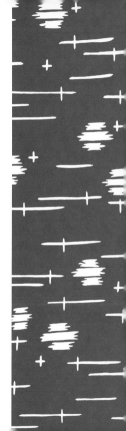

It is always possible to get back into a race if you have confidence in your ability to look like a winner. If you can exude confidence you will be perceived as someone who is in control, which can buy you the time necessary to regain your full confidence and get back up there with the leaders.

Courage, determination, and hard work are all very nice to discover in yourself; perhaps not quite as nice as discovering a goldmine on your property, but twice as valuable.

While there remains, from generation to generation, those who are confident, self-controlled, and optimistic, there will always be an element of society striving to overcome the suffering they witness in the world.

You can either join the line of those asking why the world isn't a better place, or you can be the first in line of those confident and prepared enough to try and make it so.

If you can be confident about the way you
spend your time, and become confident in
your mental attitude toward life, you cannot
be perceived by others as anything other than
a confident person.

**Place your confidence in attitudes.
Attitudes create and change facts.**

Believe and act as if it were impossible to fail, and you might just discover it comes true.

The moon is still in the sky: be confident of this. A new day will begin and there will soon be no trace of the dream called yesterday.

What the caterpillar calls the end, the rest of the world calls a butterfly.

Lao Tzu

A healthy attitude is contagious. Some wait to catch it from others; others become the carriers.

When people can live together, confident of each other's friendship and mutual trust, there is nothing that cannot be achieved within that community from the accumulated skills and abilities of those who make it up.

One comes to believe whatever one repeats to oneself sufficiently often, whether the statement is true or false. It comes to be the dominating thought in one's mind. This can be used for or against a person, but can certainly help break down any personal barriers that exist, which have been barring the way to personal confidence.

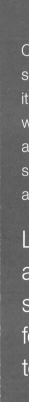

Confidence doesn't only serve you well privately, it can help those you work with or for, and inspire the ability, confidence, and self-esteem of the people around you.

Learn to appreciate successful people for what they can teach you.

Take a good and realistic look at yourself from time to time. What do you consider to be your strengths and where do you think your weaknesses lie?

If you are ashamed of your looks, work to change them to how you'd like them to be. Start with a good hairstyle, some new shoes, a sauna, or even a massage!

Why is the world such a dangerous place? It is not because of those who do evil, but because so many are prepared to stand by, look on, and do nothing to stop it. To be confident of a safer world, one must make a stand to change this.

Building self-confidence is like constructing a bridge: rush it and it will probably collapse; get the balance right and you'll not only be able to cross it safely once, but over and over again, each time with more impressive loads and occasionally with friends and followers.

How will you know when others have confidence in you? When you suddenly discover that people willingly do exactly what you want them to do for you.

Prepare yourself for whatever may befall you. Do not allow your self-esteem and self-confidence to depend solely upon any one thing, or you are in for a very hard fall should you lose that thing, whether it is a job, a person, a place, or an object.

Look in the mirror and say aloud: "I was born to win!"

Strive to align your actions with your convictions.

Suddenly you will find yourself wondering why all that shyness you once had has vanished and you have become friendly and outgoing. It is because you are confident.

You will know confidence when it arrives: it will be the force that is driving you toward your dreams.

Bear no malice toward those who did not support you or show faith in all you did.

A confidence trick is just the work of one person's confidence matched against another's. Perhaps it is better to be fooled and to learn from it than to be constantly suspicious.

It is impossible to go through life having everybody like you. Some will in fact dislike you, but that's okay.

These days I find I have far more respect for a greater number of people than ever before—they've earned it! And what's more, I too seem to be daily receiving greater respect from more and more people—I've earned it!

Become more open-minded. Become interested in new ideas, get involved in meeting and understanding new people.

A person cannot directly choose his circumstances, but he can choose his thoughts, and so indirectly, yet surely, shape his circumstances.

Some team coaches like to use the analogy of snowflakes. Alone they form one of nature's most fragile objects, but together, the entire landscape changes.

There is a world of difference between a good leader and a boss: one breeds confidence; the other fear and loathing.

The secret of culture is to learn. Remember that the path to confidence is a journey.

Confident people are objective. They will evaluate themselves realistically, appreciating their achievements and learning from their mistakes.

With the right mindset, we can begin to discover our true feelings about ourselves, which are not feelings based upon how we feel we are being perceived by society at large.

If you don't ask, you don't get. Good people will happily help you and encourage you, if only you ask them.

Naturally confident people don't have to advertise how good they are. It's obvious by their actions.

If your physique doesn't match your own beliefs about how you should look, change the belief.

All learning without doubt brings with it a sense of achievement and a rise in confidence—it can be a sure first step in the right direction.

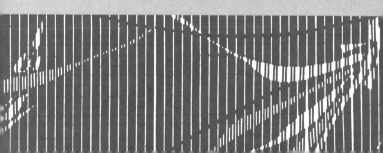

Every life is so filled with wonder, fate, irresistible and unknown inspiration, that no two of us live it in exactly the same way. Therefore we must get to know ourselves to get the most out of it.

Loss of self-esteem and confidence can exacerbate social exclusion, particularly where it comes as a consequence of stigma and discrimination.

Some virtues that arise from Nature degenerate into vices; others which are acquired, are rarely perfect. Reason teaches us to manage our estate and our confidence, while Nature provides each of us with the potential for goodness and valor.

The confidence we have in ourselves arises in a great measure from that confidence we have in others.

A confident person is so in attitude, not only in feats, not only on set days and occasions, but at all hours, even in repose.

Hope feeds off hope.

Don't be fooled by those who strut around with a capable and superior look, for these are also the traits that accompany mediocrity.

Confidence becomes faith when you believe in a thing, and believe in it all the way.

Surround yourself with confident people and learn from their example.

Only fools ignore wisdom. All they can ever be confident about is that they will suffer the consequences of their actions, which is a very painful method of learning.

Confident people recognize that much of the power to achieve and maintain their well-being lies within themselves, and that desires that are allowed to run unchecked often lead to ruin.

Begin your search for self-confidence within yourself; seek it elsewhere and you will fail.

What is "being confident"?
It is being able to talk well
with people, having belief in
your ability, not holding
yourself back, and others
trusting you to do what
must be done.

Whoever does not respect
confidence is unlikely to discover
happiness on their life-path.

When you're considering how to dress for work, ask yourself how you want to be perceived. Are colleagues likely to question your judgment and ability if you wear certain clothes? Dress effectively.

If you believe you can, then you will. Have confidence in your abilities.

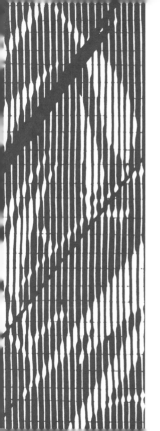

Most leaders inspire others to have confidence in them; a great leader inspires others to have confidence in themselves.

Confidence is the foundation of peace and friendship. If we give it, we will receive it.

Confidence and courage
cannot be bought:
they come through preparation
and practice.

**What do top people have?
Courage, confidence, and a
risk-seeking profile, which
is the formula that most
employers need.**

Do not devote time to disparaging others. Nobody benefits by it; it only serves to reduce confidence and increase discontent.

Friendship brings great confidence into our lives, which comes from knowing that their help will be there should we need it.

If you like a man's laugh before you know anything of him, you may say with confidence that he is a good man.

Fyodor Dostoevsky

People who appear to have an answer for everything, and wish to give the impression that they know everything, are regularly heard repeating that which they have heard others say.

Confidence is that exuberant feeling one experiences when the mind embarks on great and honorable courses with hope, certainty, and trust in itself.

In society, the link between acquaintance and friendship is confidence.

It is obviously possible to have confidence in something which we do not fully understand—this we call our faith, and religion and politics would not exist without it.

Nothing flatters our pride so much as the confidence of the great, because we regard it as the result of our worth.

A confident mind sees things as they should be seen, appraises their proper value, and turns them to its own advantage.

A confident mind adheres firmly to its own opinions only having considered the force, weight, and repercussions of outside opinions that would seek to sway it.

Confidence doesn't come from trying to impress others. It comes from doing the right thing at the right time, and for the right reasons.

Don't be discouraged. It's often the last key in the bunch that opens the lock.

Don't worry about defeat. This can be turned around to victory. But giving up—well, that makes things permanent!

**For every minute spent organizing,
an hour is earned.**

You are absolutely right,
whether you think you can
or whether you think you can't.

**When one becomes certain
of one's own motives,
one can choose to
advance or retreat
with confidence.**

You can always walk away in confidence when you know you do not have anything left to give.

Be brave: have confidence in your ability, then be tough enough to follow through.

Do everything with as much confidence as you can muster, especially when you lose and lose again. Because losing has a danger of becoming a habit and only self-confidence will break it.

Strength is less about muscle and more about the made-up mind. It does not come from physical capacity: it comes from an indomitable will.

The good or ill of a man lies within his own will.

The man who can drive himself further once the effort gets painful is the man who will win.

Being popular has less to do with looks and more to do with the magnetism of a confident attitude.

Self-determination is fine when tempered by self-control.

Our mission in life is not to merely try and succeed, but to learn to fail in good spirits, confident that we can always try again.

With confidence you can raise your gaze from your shadow on the ground and feel the sun on your face; your shadow will always be there, you can be confident of that.

When you are confident you will still have your limitations, but you will find that they will no longer worry you. Yearnings that once overwhelmed you become vague and momentary.

Life is a series of sprints and races against opponents, time, and yourself.

The control center of your life is your attitude. The person who sends out positive thoughts activates the world around him positively.

First let yourself know what you would be;
then do what you have to do.

**For success,
attitude is equally
as important as ability.**

Which are you? The person
who says, "I don't know" or
the person who says, "I'll
find out"?

Be confident in your actions—every journey, without exception, begins with the first step. A single step can make the world of difference.

Do not worry that no one knows of you; seek to be worth knowing.

There are three kinds of people: those who confidently roll up their sleeves and get stuck in; those who stick their noses in the air and turn away; and those who don't stick around at all.

The greatest truth anyone can come to know with total confidence is that time is precious and should never be wasted.

To tread on someone's hope is to tread on their dreams.

How can we ever hope to know the universe and be confident of its secrets and ways when we have such a difficult time coming to know and understand our own?

He who considers doing good knocks at the gate. He who is confident of doing good finds the door open and enters.

The Spirit Within

The "fight to the finish" spirit within us is the one characteristic we must possess if we are to face the future as confident finishers.

Try to imagine that everyone you meet through life is fighting an even harder battle than your own.

Be thankful each and every day. Even if you feel you haven't learned a lot, be confident that you will have learned a little.

The great creator gave you a body that can withstand practically anything, and a spirit to overcome the greatest adversity.

Research brings confidence—use the library or the internet to find out how to get the type of work you wish for, or how to set up home in the country of your choice.

Confidence is a virtue more persecuted by those without it than those with it.

The most confident among us are those who have known both gain and loss.

There is nothing more dreadful than the habit of doubt. Doubt undermines confidence and separates people.

Don't try and suit everybody all the time.

Every war, no matter how it might have been justified, is still a crime, and you can be confident of that fact.

All wrongdoing arises because of what goes on in the minds of men.

If a man lives a confident life, there is little that can harm him.

Hatred will not cease by administering hatred, but you can be confident that by administering love, it can.

The world is full of willing people, some willing to work at making this a better world and the rest willing to sit back and let them get on with it.

Confident people do not believe in anything simply because it is found written in religious books.

There are no shortcuts
to any place worth going.

The world can indeed seem like a dream, and
the treasures of the world are an alluring mirage,
but with confidence we can live that dream.

**See all living beings as
your father or mother,
and love them as if
you were their child.**

It doesn't take confidence to kill an insect
or hurt an animal; it only takes cruelty.

Every being who is
born will be hailed
as essential.

You, as much as anybody in the entire universe, deserve your own love and affection.

With our thoughts, we make the world we live in; with confident and pure thoughts, we make it a safer, more peaceful place to be.

Words of praise and fame serve only to beguile us; therefore blow them away.

Change the way you speak about yourself. Putting yourself down spoils your self-image.

Dwell with confidence, for what you dwell on can make the world of difference.

The plans you make can change everything now and forever.

When you engage in systematic, purposeful action, using and stretching your abilities to the maximum, you cannot help but feel positive and confident.

In order to excel, you must be completely dedicated to your chosen path, be prepared to work hard, and always accept constructive criticism.

Confidence demands dedication, at the very least to yourself.

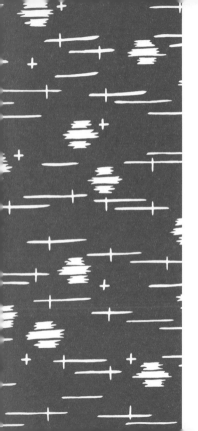

From the very first fire that was lit, smoke instinctively knew from Nature that it had the confidence and ability to fly.

Confidence satisfies all our expectations and everything immediately seems to fall into place.

You will never be able to talk confidently if you never allow your mouth to open and let the words fall out.

For years you have passed the receptionist at your place of work and only ever mumbled a pitiful "Morning." Pick your moment, smile, and try instead, "Isn't it just the most beautiful morning out there?" and invite a response before moving on.

There needs but one wise man in a company, and all are wise.

Being confident is a skill you can learn—it's as easy as riding a bike or learning to sing. These capabilities lie in wait within us all.

Don't be afraid to try new approaches to achieve successful outcomes in your personal life, relationships, and career.

**A confident leader fixes mistakes
without affixing blame.**

One type of confidence bathes in the
glory of status and possession; the
other comes from realizing that one is
privileged enough to have a duty in life
and the ability to do it.

**The mother who knows she can help her
child with homework may have more
confidence than the chairman who
doesn't know how to help his company.**

The greatest glory of having a confident and strong character is in employing it to affront the horrors of depravity.

Inestimable are those to whom we can say what we cannot say to ourselves.

To live we must conquer incessantly; we must have the courage to be happy.

Henri Frederic Amiel

True confidence comes from knowing that we can function effectively in whatever we encounter.

Don't try and hog conversations, but do feel confident enough to develop your share of them.

Every accomplishment starts with the decision to try.

**Open your door to confidence—
it can illuminate the darkest house
with inspiring thoughts.**

Success is a very tall ladder.
Its rungs are formed from
strength of character,
courage and conviction,
tenacity and fortitude,
vision and fearlessness.
But the footing that supports it,
and without which it would certainly
tumble, is confidence.

With ability, motivation, and the right attitude, a person is capable of doing well at anything they turn their determination to.

It will always remain a mystery to the minority why it should be that the majority have little or no willpower, nor the ambition to develop themselves.

Great people have in common an immense belief in themselves and in their mission.

Dressing confidently makes one of the most effective statements about us.

Confidence grows with age and experience. As people grow older, it is harder and harder to frighten them.

Make each person you meet in life feel important, and you will be made to feel more and more important by them.

Only those who are willing to improve themselves can shake off the ties that bind them.

Once you've started to build your self-esteem, you'll find your increased confidence affecting the way you act in the rest of your life.

Choose the company of those who are secure in their self-belief, but quiet enough about it for you to feel just as secure about your own.

If others can see that you are willing to deal, so they will be more willing to deal with you.

So what if you discover that your own strength is unequal to some task—it does not mean that it is beyond the powers of all.

The pessimist sees only the dark side of the clouds in the sky; the philosopher both sides; the optimist is too busy confidently leaping from cloud to cloud to notice what the others think.

Call me confident but never brave. Just because I am resistant to fear, do not mistake it for an absence of fear.

If you wish to go to your grave confident that history will look upon you kindly, dedicate your life to good, honest works and fair play.

If constructive thoughts are planted, positive outcomes will grow.

You can waste an entire lifetime trying to reach the unreachable star, but take pride in the fact that you even considered it and had the confidence to listen to reason.

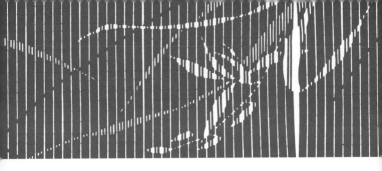

Avoid anybody who drains you of your self-esteem through put-downs or by trying to make you look or feel inferior. You don't need them in your life.

There's no scarcity of opportunity to make a living at what you love, only a scarcity of resolve to make it happen.

Since man developed the capacity for thought, he has tried to define self-esteem and confidence.

We will know instinctively when the confidence we seek draws near, as everything will fall into place.

The prominent and recent thinkers of modern times seem to forget that at some time in the past a man armed with only a stick, stood up to a dinosaur.

Confidence exists for everyone equally.

Facts are always important, but our attitude toward them is crucial, and can determine a successful or failed outcome.

No person can be entirely confident that the beliefs they are prepared to fight for contain the whole truth and nothing but the truth—one has to search more deeply.

The real voyage of discovery is having the confidence to look through new eyes.

When we feel we are worthy and valued, we participate more and try new things, and our confidence grows.

Start taking notice of the good things about yourself.

Nobody who has set out to discover their confidence has not enjoyed the experience.

Confidence allows us a sense of belonging and inspires us to contribute more to the make-up of this world. If only leaders could see the importance of helping people to preserve these fundamental human rights, they could repair much of the world's damage in no time at all.

Look in the mirror and say aloud:
"My age is an advantage to me."

**Believe in yourself and trust that
even when you are not able to work
at your very best, you will get
through what needs to be done.**

Learn to look at people
when you talk to them.

Instead of waiting for the right circumstances,
create them.

Suddenly you will find that you have forgiven yourself for being so self-critical all this time.

Thrive on deadlines and the challenges they set. Prove to yourself and others what you are capable of.

Winning is not everything. Place your confidence in your effort to try and win.

Have no fear of criticism and even welcome it into your life. Some, no matter how negative, will be useful, objective, informative, and possibly inspiring; the rest can simply be regarded as nonsense.

Each difficulty and problem you face up to and resolve makes you stronger and wiser.

Everybody's self-esteem levels fluctuate because the demands of every human life are never constant.

To succeed at the level you want to, you have to be serious about it.

Many of us are guilty of overdramatizing situations. Have you ever heard yourself telling someone you totally panicked when the truth is that at the time you experienced some anxiety?

In anything decisive, it is the one who takes the initiative who holds the advantage.

Weigh up your chances, calculate the risks, and consider your ability to deal with them. Then, and only then, can you make plans with any confidence.

Win the confidence of those around you and anything becomes possible; lose confidence in yourself and those around you will quickly recognize it.

First thing every morning, say out loud: "I believe in me."

When you brush your teeth, repeat in your mind over and over again: "Every day, in every way, I'm getting better and better."

If you seek courage, find your own inner reserves; do not hope to find in yourself the courage of others.

The only thing more powerful than the sun is the human spirit when it is on fire.

Cast off and sail away from the safe harbor. Let your sails catch the winds and take you where you've never dared to go!

The only thing that stands
between a man and what
he wants from life is often
merely the will to try it and
the faith to believe it is possible.

Always apply the best of yourself to the task at hand, and then you can walk away with confidence.

Mankind was put on this earth to do good for others; the trouble is that most of the others haven't got a clue what they were put on this earth for!

One of the greatest moments in anybody's developing experience is when he no longer tries to hide from himself but determines to get acquainted with himself as he really is.

There would be no progress in this world if it were not for certain individuals who refuse to accept that what they know in their hearts to be right cannot be done.

We all age, but one can be confident of never growing old while one retains the capacity to be as fascinated as a curious child at the world and everything in it.

Consider the butterfly. It counts its life not in years or days, but lives it in moments and is still confident of having time enough.

One can soar on the wings of confidence, but don't make each flight an ego trip—the higher you get, the smaller you're likely to appear to those still on the ground!

Truths are easy to understand once they are discovered; but who among us has the confidence to go out there and discover them?

We should live in confidence of the fact that if we do not cause trouble for anyone else, there will be no cause for them to trouble us.

Direct the course of your life by reason, not chance, and only then can you be confident of living a reasonable life.

Humanity is a confident mutual agreement, among men and women, not to inflict or allow harm to befall each other.

The just man is the freest of anyone from anxiety; but the unjust man is perpetually haunted by it.

The world is a stage, so don't slink into the shadows. Come out into the limelight and be seen. Let your voice ring out and your gestures be clear.

There is no chance, no destiny, no fate that can hinder or control the firm resolve of a determined soul.

Some seek greatness, fame, and high status—believing it will protect them from ever lacking confidence—only to discover that they have even less confidence than they had when they started.

Do not convince yourself that you lack confidence. You are simply unripe, and have not yet come to know yourself.

Say to yourself: "I am a confident individual and I feel optimistic and motivated."

Always add something to your ensemble that makes the statement "I am happy to be noticed."

When you know your strengths and the accumulated strengths of others around you who can be called upon, you can make any decision with great confidence.

If a decision you took to bed with you looks as good the next morning, put it into action!

If you can learn to handle failure and accept that mistakes often happen, you can shift any associated negativity into a new, more positive light.

If you act as though you lack confidence, other people will pick up on it and react to that.

There is no great talent without great willpower.

Our chief want in life is somebody who'll make us do what we can. We'll find that someone either in the shape of a friend or within ourselves.

Use little positive statements about yourself as often as possible. Make a list of them and repeat them to yourself regularly.

Without at least a modest confidence in your abilities, you cannot expect to be successful or happy. So have a little faith and start believing in yourself.

Don't
Minimize
your
Contribution

Have confidence in your contribution to civilization—even birds of a single note help to make up the harmony of the forest.

When we envy others,
we sacrifice our own
peace of mind.

All that we are is the result of what we have thought. All that we are arises with our thoughts. With our thoughts, we make our world.

If we speak and act with the confidence that our thoughts are pure, happiness will follow us through life.

We can be confident that, just as with everything else, we never exist entirely alone—our lives are lived in relation to all things.

Confidence only tells us the way. It is then up to us to sweat out the task.

Our attitude is an expression of our values, beliefs, and expectations.

It is not enough to believe everything one is told merely out of respect. Each of us should become a lamp unto ourselves.

If we are diligent in our duties and seek knowledge and understanding, we will discover the self-confidence that will liberate us and become our refuge for a lifetime.

Confident people accept and live up to anything that agrees with reason and is conducive to the benefit of one and all.

Inward calm is difficult to maintain when we are unable to replenish our physical strength and relax our mind.

People become remarkable from the first moment they begin to believe that they can do something.

Bad men never appreciate kindnesses shown them; wise men appreciate and are grateful.

Discover your work and then, with all your heart, give yourself to it.

Whatever you find to be kind, conducive to the good, benefit, and welfare of all beings, believe it and cling to it, and with confidence take it as your guide.

Fill your life with people who respect you and treat you well.

Just because you feel confident does not mean you have to attend every argument you are invited to.

True prosperity is the result of well placed confidence in ourselves and our fellow man.

Conflict can deepen or damage a relationship, depending on the attitude of those caught up in it.

When one feels tranquil, one finds
pleasure in listening to good teachings.

**You will have to depart this world
leaving everything behind,
so do not be attached to anything.
Make your attachments to yourself
and those around you.**

**When you commit yourself
to you, you commit yourself
to success!**

It is completely meaningless
to put effort into activities
that have no essence.

**The gain in self-confidence after
having accomplished a tiresome
labor is immense.**

It's not what happens to you,
but how you react to it that matters.

If you think: "I'll never make the deadline," you're likely to be swamped by anxiety and panic. Instead think: "Okay, I am under pressure, but I have the skills I need to complete this," and you're far more likely to remain in control and pull it off.

Learn to recognize and appreciate all your accomplishments.

Time isn't found:
you need to have the
confidence to make it or
take it from somewhere else.

History has proved that a confident
attitude is more important than
appearance or what has gone before.

**A person's confidence stretches
beyond the extent of their
education, their wealth, or their
circumstances.**

Self-confidence comes to us as the result of having done all the things we momentarily feared doing.

Self-confidence is a trail of successful experiences that stretches back through our lives.

Say to yourself: "I am a confident individual and I don't mind who knows it!"

Manage your mind—defeat all of your negative self-talk.

When the going gets tough, give someone what you'd wish to receive yourself: a pat on the back, an encouraging smile, and a simple "You can do it!"

It is better not to trust completely in the advice of a person in difficulties, but this does not mean that one cannot place confidence in their capabilities.

Happiness depends upon ourselves and is the offspring of confidence.

Promise yourself that you are absolutely committed to completing each journey you begin.

The person who remains cool and focused while getting on with the task at hand is perceived as a confident person of quality amid the flurry of those others whose approach is one of haste.

A life that is full of disturbance and confusion must be put back on track by focusing on an achievable goal.

Suddenly you will find yourself wondering why you are not afraid to admit your mistakes. It is because you are confident.

Every morning, say aloud: "I welcome and embrace the challenges of this new day and the risks it presents to me."

Confidence puts a twinkle in the eye, a tone in the voice, and a spring in the step.

If we are able to function as self-efficient beings in terms of our actions and behavior, this has a positive, domino effect on how we perceive ourselves. This is where our self-respect comes from.

Say to yourself: "I am a confident individual and I go out of my way to try and make the people around me feel secure."

Self-esteem and confidence in individuals has a direct effect on their inclusion and achievement. When our levels are low, we put up a barrier to stop ourselves from taking up opportunities and the only way to raise it is to change our attitude.

Look in the mirror and say aloud: "I am often at my best under pressure."

If one has determination, things will get done.

Positive thinking will enable you to do everything better than with negative thinking.

The freedom to be your best means nothing unless you are willing to do your best.

The men who succeed are the efficient few.

Life is not filled with hopeless situations, but with people whose attitudes are hopeless. With confidence one can set about changing all that.

Tell yourself that you are a confident individual and do not take unnecessary risks; you are forward-looking and plan ahead.

What we see mainly depends upon what it is we are looking for.

Learn to self-conquest, persevere thus for a time, and you will perceive very clearly the advantage which you gain from it.

St. Teresa of Avila

Life at any time can become difficult. Life at any time can become easy. It all depends upon how one adjusts oneself to life.

When things seem to go wrong it isn't defeat. Accept that your plans are not yet absolutely right. Redesign them and set out again.

Attitude controls our lives for good or bad, and one cannot be confident of a peaceful and productive outcome until this great force is harnessed.

Being "big" doesn't depend on height or status. It is the crown worn by those who have the ability to make all of us feel bigger when we are in their company.

Rarely has anyone without confidence won at anything. If and when they have, only a small percentage of them turn their good luck into a first step toward confidence.

Of all the attitudes we can acquire, surely gratitude is the most important and by far the most life-changing.

A confident mental attitude is more important than mental capacity alone.

Your self-esteem depends upon accepting yourself unconditionally.

Confidence makes us feel safe and secure. We learn to trust ourselves and when to place our trust in others.

Confidence is difficult to find where there is no sense of purpose.

If you wish to give children the very best present of all, let them know that you have confidence in their abilities.

Be confident of having the freedom to form a positive attitude toward whatever circumstances you find yourself placed in.

Sometimes you can win people and influence situations with your attitude much more easily than you can with your aptitude.

With the right confidence
and encouragement,
one person can bring
sunshine into everybody's day.

More powerful than the will to win
is the confidence to begin.

File in your memory several images of plight and daily call them to the forefront of your mind while repeating to yourself: "I am a lucky person."

To discover what it means to achieve goals, start modestly by setting small, achievable ones —like giving up one cup of coffee a day for a week. If you succeed in achieving your goal, celebrate it!

Remember that potential bosses and suitors want to be around people they can relate to.

If a person gets their attitude toward themselves straight, it will help straighten out almost every other area in their life.

Vanity is insatiable.

Suddenly you will find yourself wondering why setbacks seem to simply roll off your back. It is because you are confident.

When you are confident enough to consider the lives of the many people in the world who are worse off than you, and realize your own comparative good fortune, any dissatisfaction on your part soon becomes unwarranted.

As our confidence grows, so too does the range of new and exciting challenges that present themselves to us.

The confident find pleasure and contentment in what they do.

Don't try and be as sexy as your idol. Try and be someone your idol might be interested in meeting…. Try being yourself.

At each stage of your confidence-building quest, you will achieve new and positive things. Celebrate these and pause occasionally to reflect how they came to be.

Foresight and friendship equal happiness.

Confident people do not dwell on things that they do not have. They are not troubled by envy.

Some are confident enough to rule nations, yet are enslaved by their own lustful desires. True self-confidence is reached when we can also exercise self-control.

Be generous to others with your time, expertise, and knowledge, but also know when it is time to say no.

Confident people know that whatever is needed to live happily can be found without great struggle or sacrifice, and will never allow themselves to be taken in by those whose mission in life it is to make people feel they need the things they don't.

Confident people know their natural limits, beyond which one can have "too much of a good thing."

Be confident in the knowledge that the pains that result from excess are many and can haunt for a lifetime.

Confident people recognize that human instinct leads the majority to suffer and toil, and know how and when to ignore their own basic animal nature and social custom for the sake of good sense and reason.

Confident people know how and when to be flexible, and recognize that it is wise to take an occasional break from day-to-day routine.

The richest fools are often miserable.

A confident character is developed by swimming against the full current of life.

Being confident does not mean that you will not be confronted in life with things that will bring you great pain and heartbreak, but you do not bring these things about and you can be confident that you will be able to pick up the pieces afterward.

If you keep your desires within the natural limits set by Nature, even poverty will seem like great wealth to you.

Purge yourself of all those things that tether you to the ground.

You cannot change your history, but you can leave it behind you and resolve to make a better and different future.

The hopes of those who are confident are attainable, while the daydreams of those who are not will remain impossible until they get in touch with their self-confidence.

Socialize and develop your confidence in relating to others.

Confident people do not tend
to waste their lives in fear.

**Tough times never last,
but tough people do.**

Twenty years from now you will be
more disappointed by the things that
you didn't do than by the ones you did.

The difference between the impossible and
the possible lies in a person's determination.

Many home and work relationships are guilty of stripping away the confidence people had before they entered into them. If this happens, one must weigh up which is more important and have the confidence to either stay and work on it or turn and walk away.

When people give to someone else they raise not only their own self-esteem, by knowing they are able to give, but also the self-confidence of the receiver, who realizes they are worth giving to.

Never punish yourself over honest mistakes. The only way to correct all of our mistakes in life is to live it twice.

History is filled with examples of important accomplishments by people who kept trying even when there seemed to be little or no hope at all.

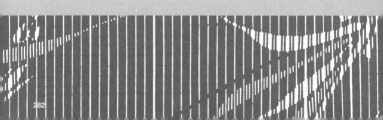

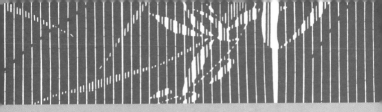

Ask the questions you cannot answer; attempt the tasks you believe you cannot achieve. Only then will you truly know what you are capable of.

Life takes on a whole new set of meanings the moment we become motivated.

It is a common belief that we will all look back on our life from our deathbed. If only this could motivate us to strive to live as we would have wished to have lived from that viewpoint.

Go forward confidently, energetically attacking problems, and you can expect favorable outcomes.

Not until you allow yourself will you ever achieve a sense of belonging. It is up to you to include yourself in your life.

Happiness is an attitude of mind, born of the simple determination to be happy regardless of all circumstances, and the confidence that one can be.

When you present yourself well, it makes the statement that you believe you are worth it.

Courage is not about the absence of fear: it is about remaining confident and resisting being afraid. Every true hero has cowardice within, but masters that fear and goes onward regardless of it.

Be grateful for every step forward you can take with confidence in this life, for you will have begun a journey to something better than things are now.

Spot the confident people— they exude an aura of being sure without being cocky.

Imagine having the confidence of everybody around you for what it is you are about to do.

If you start by doing what is necessary and then move on to doing what is possible, soon you will discover you are doing what at first seemed impossible.

People who are not confident spend their lives defending their wrongs more than their rights.

If you wish to get to the very essence of anything with accuracy, you will have to be prepared to ask intelligent questions and put aside your assumptions.

The mind and the body do not shun pleasure voluntarily, and optimal life requires self-control.

Know your limits and clearly state the need for more resources from your family, friends, colleagues, or managers. This is called efficiency!

Start Where
You Are

With the right amount of curiosity, some courage, constancy, and above all, confidence, dreams can be made to come true.

To be idle is a short road to death and to be diligent is a way of life. Foolish people are idle; wise people are diligent.

Suddenly you will find yourself wondering why you are able to see beyond all problems to what lies beyond. It is because you are confident.

Confidence, once we have discovered it in ourselves and understand its ways, will remain with us and, like our shadow, never leave our side.

Confidence
does not
dwell in
the past,
nor does
it dwell upon
the future.
It concentrates
the mind
on the
present
moment.

Learn to take the time required to do things correctly.

Develop your ability to endure, for endurance is one of the most difficult disciplines, but with it one can live in great confidence, for it is to the one who endures that the final victory comes.

Try to know what leads you forward and what it is that holds you back. Then you can choose the path that will lead you to confidence and wisdom.

Confident people do not believe in traditions simply because they have been handed down for many generations.

Everything is changeable; nothing remains without change.

Some people are difficult to deal with.
It's just their way. Reward them
with your own pleasantness when
they are not being difficult, and they
will soon become confident in their new
and better ways.

**Friendship is the only cure for
hatred, the only guarantee of peace.**

**Life is a matter of acceptance and
avoidance; where you are reluctant to
make your choice there will always be a
conflict of confidence.**

To strive to keep the body in good health is important. But most vital is to keep the mind strong, clear, and confident.

Whatever words we utter should be chosen with confidence and great care, for people will hear them and be influenced by them for good or ill.

Share with confidence.
Happiness never decreases
by being shared.

First direct
yourself in
the way you
should go.
Only then
should you
instruct others.
Be prepared
to open yourself
to life and live
it with concern
for all beings.

Avoid friends who cause you to increase delusions, and place your confidence instead in those who would increase your virtue.

Do not contemplate your own good qualities, but contemplate the good qualities of others, and respect all.

Confident people inspire others and therefore confidence carries with it certain responsibilities. You can never know when your life becomes someone else's roadmap.

In the great negotiation that we call life, we must learn to build bridges swiftly and efficiently. We are all part of something someone wants, so we should learn what it is we can actually offer and then do so with confidence.

Study Nature: from her we can discern the limits of things and come away confident in our better understanding of the ways of life.

More than 90 percent of the catastrophes
that we imagine turn out to be nothing but
painted demons in our mind.

A confident mind
has an easy breath.

You are never alone.

Don't just take your word for it.
Find out what your friends think
are your strengths and weaknesses.

Look at the interaction between a stream and a rock lying in the water. Which wins? The rock remains firm, resilient, and solid but gets nowhere; given time the stream will wear it down through sheer perseverance, not strength.

Be confident, but never take anything for granted.

Appearing confident in the workplace can be challenging, especially when there are so many corporate "gods" milling about, full of themselves.
How did they get there?
Well they probably went to one of their superiors one day and said, "I was up all night thinking about that merger you pulled off. It was sheer genius. I'd have probably done it differently, but what you did has opened my mind to a whole new world of possibilities. Thanks."

Confident people not only develop self-esteem but also a sense of responsibility and accountability.

Add a flourish to your day by reading a different paper, taking a different route, saying "Hi" to someone you have never spoken to before.

When you meet people, say under your breath: "I am a confident individual and I am not afraid to look people in the eye."

Never overgeneralize on the basis of a single unfortunate experience. Just because you have had one driving accident it doesn't make you a bad driver; just because one relationship broke up doesn't mean you are bad at relationships. The chances of circumstances ever being absolutely the same are so incredibly low that only a fool would gamble on them.

Confident people tend to be able to find comfort and ease in any surroundings.

When we are clear about our strengths and weaknesses, we start to become more confident about what constitutes opportunity and threat in our lives.

It is a well known historical fact that no matter what your gender, those who are confident of their abilities are more likely to succeed than those who may be much more competent, talented, or industrious, but who lack confidence.

Whoever we are, there will always be someone else who thinks we are perfect.

Confidence which is brought about by reflection is noblest; confidence which is brought about by imitation is the easiest; confidence that comes from experience is often the most bitter.

The power and status we might achieve may provide us with some protection from others who would see us harmed or overthrown. But nothing can match the security we get from our own peace of mind.

If you only apply yourself on the days you feel good, little will be achieved in your lifetime. It often takes the starting of something, despite feeling negative, to generate the positivism that will encourage good feelings and lead to achievement.

Whoever you are, there is a hole in this world that only your life can fill.

If we can use affirmations to jump-start our self-belief we should soon be able to possess the deep conviction necessary to start making things happen.

With the right focus and determination, developing your self-confidence can be swift and fun. But first make a pact with yourself that you have the determination to see it through.

You can defeat a confident person, but not destroy them.

Confidence is our ability to think, to cope with the basic challenges of life, and our entitlement to be happy and successful.

Look in the mirror and say aloud:
"I can successfully handle any
challenge that comes my way."

Learn to think fast
on your feet.

The difference between a successful team and others is not a lack of strength or knowledge—it simply boils down to some individuals' lack of will.

More often than not, it is the very thing that we have difficulty in expressing that runs our lives.

Just go out there as confidently as you can and do the best you can.

Knowing is not enough; we must apply. Willing is not enough; we must do.

It is superficial and dastardly to begin upon a thing, then run away from it discouraged on meeting with some difficulty. We each have within us the capacity (or know someone with it), if only we would employ it.

Great works are performed not by strength, but perseverance. Armed with determination, diligence, and skill, one can undertake most things with confidence.

Have confidence in your own common sense.

There is nothing wrong with trying new ways, and no loss of face if they fail. Admit they were wrong and try something different.

Those who refuse to accept anything but the very best very often seem to get it.

Most doubts evaporate harmlessly under close scrutiny; those that don't represent risks and need carefully planned management.

One can swiftly get to recognize where to place one's confidence. I would rather place mine in a determined mechanic with a single wrench than a wastrel with a whole set of tools.

Failure suggests that our determination to succeed was perhaps not strong enough.

Everybody at some time feels awkward, out of their depth and lost without anything to say. That's why world leaders have scriptwriters.

There is danger in depending upon our relationships to fill the gaps in our being created by our own low self-esteem. If we can't bring ourselves to love ourselves, how can we expect others to?

Sometimes a relationship breaks down and our confidence goes out of the window with it. The most common mistake is to rush out and immediately jump into another relationship in an attempt to provide a momentary boost.

The will to do springs from the knowledge that we can do.

Want to lose weight? Do some simple exercises while you are planning something else and you'll achieve two things at once!

A genius is someone who is supremely confident of their own belief that what is true within their heart is also true for all of mankind.

Confidence is the fuel for success.

If you know in your heart of hearts that certain things are not right for you, stop chasing after them and replace them with things that are better suited and obtainable.

To those whose confidence has added new sciences, to those whose confidence has refined life, to those whose confidence has resulted in freedom and justice; to each great heart and genius we owe our own confidence.

Confidence owes as much to being open to all the questions as it does to knowing many of the answers.

If you try to stretch yourself to new limits and mess up on the way, don't let it bruise your confidence.

Some desires are natural and necessary; some desires are natural but not necessary; and others neither natural nor necessary.

Self-respect, the moment you develop it, permeates every aspect of your life.

There can be no self-respect without self-trust. With both in place you can guarantee you are in for a confident and happy life.

There's no substitute for hard work.

Forget superstition and luck. The happy conditions of life may be had on the same terms as occur in Nature. Their attraction for us is the pledge that they are within our reach.

While others were sitting around, saying among themselves it couldn't be done, it was done.

Before any meeting, audition, interview, or dealing with a difficult person, give yourself a moment or two to run through a mental list of your strengths and enter that meeting with all the confidence you can muster.

Will you look back on life and say, "I wish I had…" or "I'm glad that I did…"?

Vacillating people seldom succeed.
Successful men and women are
careful in reaching their decisions,
and persistent and determined
in action thereafter.

**This world has been developed
through the sheer confident
determination, courage,
faith, and endurance of a
confident few who surmounted
all the obstacles and pressed
on regardless of the odds.**

The height of your accomplishments will equal the depth of your convictions.

Success is a ladder you cannot climb with your hands in your pockets.

If you know your own mind, you'll always triumph over those who don't know theirs.

Don't sit around to wait and see what happens. Confident people get out there and make the right things happen.

The more philosophical you can become about life, the easier it is to retain your confidence.

You can handle rejection because you can always try again and again, each time with greater experience under your belt.

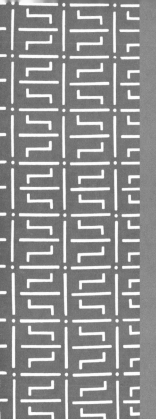

People can generally
make time for what
they choose to do;
it is the will that is
lacking, not the time.

The mind is all that
counts. You can
be whatever
you make up a
confident mind
to be.

One of the greatest boosts to self-confidence is learning something new. From astrology to parachuting, a foreign language, chess, learning to play a musical instrument, or how to cook—classes, games, and sports mean contact with others.

Suddenly you will find yourself wondering why you are able to think clearly even when you are under extreme pressure. It is because you are confident.

Our subconscious minds have no real sense of the difference between reality and an imagined thought or image. What we think about continually will eventually manifest in our lives.

We cannot always control our thoughts. We have to work hard at being able to impress our own subconscious, and only when we can will we be able to become masters of any situation.

A confident attitude is welcomingly contagious. Let others catch yours.

Confidence grants us our independence and makes for cheerful relations in home and work life, but it also brings us the desire to serve and in some way contribute to the well-being of fellow men.

When you choose to be pleasant and positive to others, you also choose how you are going to be treated by others.

Engaging in purposeful action stretches our abilities and we cannot help but feel positive and confident about ourselves.

**The best thing to do with a life
is to live it confidently.**

The choice is yours. Start
each day by preparing your
victory speech or stay in bed
and send a note of apology!

Inner confidence can influence situations and outcomes—you know you'll be fine.

Because we all get nervous we end up looking down, and everybody notices everybody else's shoes! Keep yours polished and in good repair.

A bright smile goes a long way to making us feel better about ourselves and projects a positive image to others.

Acceptance of others brings you an inner peace and tranquillity, instead of anger and resentment.

If your sword's too short, add to its length by taking one step forward.

Your confidence can quell all the doubt and negativity others hold about you.

Always ask yourself: "What do I need to know in order to make a good decision here?" If you are working in a team, put the same question out to tender among them and weigh up as much of the information as you can.

Successful folks don't just entertain thoughts— they put them to work.

Remember the carpenter's rule: measure twice, cut once.

Whether in your new life, job,
relationship, or other regime,
don't fall into the trap of trying to
succeed first time. It will only
demotivate you if you don't pull it off.

Don't worry about trying to look like
some famous icon from Hollywood.
Worry about looking like you.

He is great who is what he is from nature, and who never reminds us of others.

Our possibilities are only as great as our aspirations.

There is more confidence to be gained from developing your own individual take on fashion than from being a fashion victim.

Confidence allows us to recognize our native riches, the gifts we have, and how indispensable each of us is.

Spot the confident people —they are the sure-footed ones who meet life head-on.

Confidence opens our hearts and our minds to all the powers that constitute character. It wakes in us the feeling of worth and opens an entire new world to us.

The optimism of confident people is the quality more associated with success and happiness than any other.

Try and enjoy doing simple things successfully and well.

Forget about all the reasons why something may not work. You only need to find one good reason why it will to motivate your confidence and kick-start a new beginning.

Nothing is good or bad, but thinking makes it so.
William Shakespeare

Don't settle for finding the confidence for the immediate problem at hand, but strive to welcome confidence, to help you face bigger and better challenges for the duration of your life.

Do not consciously set
out seeking enlightenment,
or you can be confident
of never achieving it.

**Where did the confidence
arise from which drove
the honeysuckle to first
release its perfume
for all to sample?**

The more confidence we can all develop toward good, the better the world within us, and the world at large, will become.

One has to learn to get past self-doubt in order to make any decision.

If your goals are clear, positive, and your own, you are free to follow your gut reaction.

To have confidence and ignore it is like knowing what is right and not doing it. These are the worst forms of cowardice.

If we want to be happy and confident, we must first learn to prefer loving our life over our habits, and be prepared to let the habits go.

Controlling It

What we think, we become. Whenever you hold on to anger it is like holding a red-hot coal that you intend to throw at the cause of your anger, but in holding on to it, it will be your own hand that gets burned!

What happens is not as important as how you react to what happens.

What lies behind us and what lies before us are tiny matters compared to what lies within us.

All that we are is the result of what we have thought. If our thoughts remain confident, then we shall be also.

If one wishes to be confident of removing the wrongdoing from the world, one must begin by transforming minds.

Optimism means
expecting the best,
but confidence means
knowing how to handle
the best and the worst.

**Trouble is an inevitable part of life.
When it confronts you look it
straight in the eye and let it know
that it will never defeat you.**

We are all as chicks in the shell, tapping away, confident that there is a great, wonderful world outside, and a good life to be lived in it once we have broken through.

Meditation brings wisdom, and wisdom brings confidence. Where there is ignorance, there is little or no confidence to be found.

Confident people
do not believe in
anything merely on
the authority of
teachers and elders.

Certain things we will encounter in life have no reality in themselves, and are but mirages in a heat haze. Yet they will tempt those gullible enough to chase them. One must learn to stand one's ground in confidence of what is real and what is illusion.

With newfound confidence, what once seemed threatening suddenly looks serendipitous.

A happy person is not a person in a certain set of circumstances, but rather a person with a certain set of attitudes.

To conquer oneself is a greater victory than to conquer thousands in a battle.

All that we are arises with our thoughts. With our thoughts, we make the world. With confident thoughts, we create a confident world.

Thousands of candles can be lit from a single candle, and the life of that original candle will not be shortened. Let your confidence ignite the confidence of countless others.

Your body is precious.
Treat it with care,
then you can call upon it
to do extraordinary things
with confidence.

Confidence makes
everything appear easy;
nothing is easy to
the unwilling.

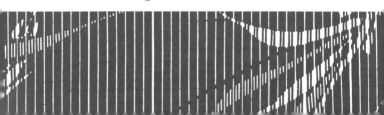

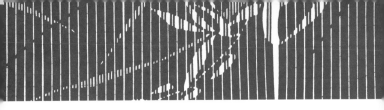

Obstacles will look large or small to you according to whether you are large or small in your outlook.

If you practice being confident with great devotion, results will arise immediately.

Don the armor of patience, free from anger. Practice concentration. Ignite the fire of the effort of application.

There are two possible sides to your character: one is a loser, the other is full of confidence. When you arrive at a party, visualize the loser you leaving. Let the confident you go in. When you want to join a conversation, visualize the loser fumbling for something of interest to say, then let the confident you step in at a good moment with something that is equally as interesting as everyone else's contribution.

There are only two ways to look good: exercise and take care of your appearance, or enrol in a club filled with people who are fatter and older than you are.

A confident human being is a resilient force to be reckoned with.

It is not because things are difficult that we do not dare, it is usually because we do not dare that they appear difficult.

Look in the mirror and say aloud: "I enjoy the challenge of learning new things."

To be confident of retaining your youthful good looks, find your own personal reasons for cheerfulness and contentment.

Confidence is born of troubles. They are vital experiences for us; they show us what we are truly capable of when the chips are down, and put our resolve to the test. Use your circumstances: don't be hindered by them.

Confidence can be fluid one moment and solid the next. For example, to remain fashionable, go with the flow, but when it comes to your principles, stand as firm as a tree.

Although fate presents the circumstances, the way you react depends upon your character.

**Your own resolution
to succeed is more
important than any
other single thing.
This is true confidence.**

Look in the mirror and say aloud:
"I am a sharp, bright, intelligent person."

Don't make happiness your goal in life. Let it come as a by-product of what you do and achieve.
This way, happiness depends less upon chance and becomes a matter of choice. This way, you can be confident that happiness will always be within your grasp.

**Look in the mirror and say aloud:
"I can learn anything quickly
and easily."**

**We can alter our lives
merely by altering our
mental attitude.**

While the political, religious, and
corporate leaders of the world
remain open-minded,
we can be confident about
the continued survival of the
human race.

Do you place your faith in the pitcher, or the water it contains? Which can you live without?

Instead of going through life always trying to change your behavior, why not dedicate some time to rethinking your beliefs.

It is not your life that needs to be changed, only your intent and actions.

Events will take their course.
There is little point in being
angry at them.

**Each experience through which
we pass operates ultimately for
our own good.**

In any sport, our strongest opponent is
neither the other player nor the other
side, but our negative internal thoughts
and voices, and the strength of our
determination to overpower them.

Confidence grows with each friend we make in life. Each friendship brings us a new level of tranquillity unknown to those without friends. Where we cannot make friends, we should avoid making enemies.

Everyday life is the way.

Zen saying

Every thing
is true
as it is.
Why dislike it?
Why hate it?

**Often the first thought
is the best thought.**

We can never be confident of a better world until we can guarantee that everyone in it has an unhindered equal opportunity to feel confident enough to engage with issues of importance —for themselves as individuals, for their communities, and for the regeneration of a peaceful and tolerant world.

With a quiet self-confidence, one always has a powerful secret weapon at one's disposal.

One discovers over time that one's entire life will shrink or expand in direct proportion to the extent of one's self-confidence.

Simply through rejecting humiliation, we can transform ourselves from psychological paralysis into powerful forces of positive change to be reckoned with.

The secret of reaping the greatest enjoyment and harvest from life is to discover how to go about it with confidence.

It is our attitude at the beginning of a challenging situation that, more than anything else, will determine the outcome. A confident outlook in an emergency can mean the difference between survival and disaster.

A person's life throws so much at them—is it any wonder their confidence levels change?
In the space of no time at all, a single individual can experience bereavement or illness; become unemployed and be forced to retrain; become a parent; win the lottery then lose it all on the stock exchange; get divorced then robbed; fall in love again and find a new job....

To think is easy.
Finding the confidence
to act in accordance
with your thinking
is key to success
and survival.

With confidence we can be happy with our achievements and optimistic for the future.

Of course we will never completely forget past difficulties, but these can be put to good use as they allow us to empathize and help others in the same boat.

Look in the mirror and say aloud: "I am willing to take intelligent risks in order to succeed."

Always give your best effort,
regardless of your role.

**Confidence is a life tool: often a
weapon, but never an ornament.**

A tutor who doesn't have the
confidence to speak up in
front of those they are
teaching comes across
as lacking in confidence.

Suddenly you will find yourself wondering why you see mistakes less as something to lament and more as good ways of learning. It is because you are confident.

Don't travel through life burdened with thoughts of failure; be willing to accept you are capable of making mistakes.

Thank goodness for confident people, for where would the world be if we didn't have so many who purport to specialize in the impossible?

Define what it is you want to be confident about and bring yourself to know what self-esteem and self-confidence mean to you.

Consciously record all changes in your self-esteem and confidence levels.

Cleanse yourself of those who imagine their chattering to be knowledge, silence to be ignorance, and affection to be art.

Take yourself less seriously and you'll laugh more often and at more things.

If you wish to have everybody's sympathy, then say: "I wish I had done better—I would have liked to have lived in Monte Carlo…" But if you want to inspire people with your confidence say: "Next time I buy a house, it's going to be in Monte Carlo!"

Nervous habits signal a lack of confidence and have to be ditched. Find out from your friends what they notice you doing and then get rid of them—the habits, not the friends!

Be confident in speaking to any individual and to any group of people, regardless of its size, that you are confronted with.

When Columbus started out, he didn't know where he was going; when he got there, he didn't know where he was; when he got back, he didn't know where he had been!

Procrastinate less and do more.

Sometimes our lack of confidence can be traced back to some trauma in our life. In such cases it can be difficult to rise above it, and it is highly advisable to take advantage of the support provided by a counselor or sympathetic friend to work through the problem.

It is possible to work faster and make fewer mistakes.

When problems arise, deal with them swiftly, effortlessly, and with greater control.

If you find doubts starting to surface, challenge each and every one calmly and rationally as they occur.

Inner confidence should not be based upon external events. Certainly we should feel good when we do well, but with inner confidence we learn to live with whatever life throws at us, and always have what we need within us to rise above any situation.

Self-confidence is the first requisite for great undertakings.

Be glad to give advice, and be happy to see it being taken by people and working for them.

One cannot hope to gain self-esteem if one places upon oneself, or is loaded with, such high expectations that one can never possibly achieve the goals alone.

The one single personality trait that most makes a person popular, attractive, and sexy to others has nothing to do with height, shape, or beauty. It is confidence. People with high self-esteem draw others to them like a magnet.

Look forward to unforeseen events and the challenges or changes in outlook they provide.

When you feel yourself falling victim to self-criticism and your confidence is fading, turn to positive thoughts.

Don't be thrown by every little thing that goes against the plan; be efficient at getting back on track with the minimum of fuss.

If you believe you can, you probably can. If you believe you won't, then you most assuredly won't.

For confidence to take hold, you've got to start remembering the good things about yourself, not the petty, negative things. Get rid of those.

Whenever we learn something new about ourselves or the world in which we live, we experience a boost in our self-esteem and confidence.

The more you venture to live greatly, the more you will find within you what it takes to get on top and remain there.

When one is filled with confidence and carrying the hope of success, one can inspire others to move mountains.

To survive a long and challenging journey, one needs a stout pair of shoes and a robust sense of humor.

Have confidence in your choice of pleasures and those which should be avoided, for some are only obtainable at the high cost of insurmountable troubles.

We must want for others, not ourselves alone.

We should be too big to take offence and too noble to give it.

Abraham Lincoln

Work on getting your thoughts and messages across in words that are clear and compelling.

We're fools whether we dance or not, so we might as well dance.

Japanese proverb

Everything becomes as easy as everything else if one begins at the beginning, and confidently proceeds in order, step by step.

There is nothing to gain from worrying yourself into ill health over trying to become something that it is impossible for you to achieve. Live a confident truth, not a lie.

If you have the confidence to throw your heart into the arena, the rest will follow.

From the very beginning you can commence stretching yourself. If you make your goals bigger and toughen up the challenges you face, the further you will increase your commitment, skills, and confidence.

It isn't failure that will break you: it is apathy.

How far can confidence go? We nurture our young with love, sympathy, and the wisdom of the ages, and accompany them right up to the gates of the arena, but they enter not with our confidence but their own, and it is on their own strengths or weaknesses they will stand or fall.

There is not a person alive in this world who is not vulnerable in some way.

Can a judge without confidence put on a brave face, weigh the arguments, and, as there must be a decision, make one that hopefully not only serves justice, but also society?

Create an enclosure of confidence around you and allow nothing into it without your permission, and certainly nothing harmful or demotivating.

You can be confident that no two minds are exactly alike— the same world that is your hell is quite probably someone else's heaven.

To change and to change for the better are two completely different things.

Your aim may be perfect and you may have all the strength needed to draw your bow, but do you have the confidence to let loose your arrows of desire?

Create a strong mental image of what you'll experience as you achieve your major goal.

Setting and achieving goals
is the key way of building
self-confidence—keep
stretching yourself, but not
too much, only as much as is
necessary to be successful.

**With some hard work
and a little confidence,
dreams can begin to come true.**

Stop allowing yourself to be influenced
against your instinct and will.

**A confident life is spent thinking about
where it wants to go and what it wants to
achieve, not dwelling on where it's been
and what it's already done.**

Nobody can perform confidently in a manner that conflicts with the way they see themselves.

Get out more and socialize, and when you do, don't be a wallflower. Mingle and make conversation, starting it if you have to—any subject will get things going. Everybody tends to wait for someone else to break the ice—seize the moment!

Listen to other people.
It is possible to determine how confident they are just by listening to what they don't say about themselves!

People will sell their souls for position and for the culture of talent, but to the interests of the confident individual, such superficial success is of little or no account.

Everyone who got where they are today had to begin where they were yesterday.

Confident people will either find a way, or make one.

Every time we take on and accomplish anything new, we learn vital lessons, the most important being that the moment we take our first step into each new arena, our initial fear and anxiety disappears, until we can take on anything with confidence.

With faith in yourself and confidence in your abilities, the only thing that stands between you and what you want to get from this life is the will to give it a try.

The quickest route to self-confidence for some is to (within reason) do something they fear.

The whole world steps aside for the people who know where they are going.

Never relinquish doing something simply because someone else is not sure of you. If you decide not to attempt to do something, then let it be because you are not sure of yourself.

If you want to feel good about your physical appearance, never compare yourself to others. It is that simple. If you want to look like the stars on screen and in the newspapers, you're going to need to be computer-enhanced and airbrushed!

What seems impossible one moment becomes possible, through confidence, in the next.

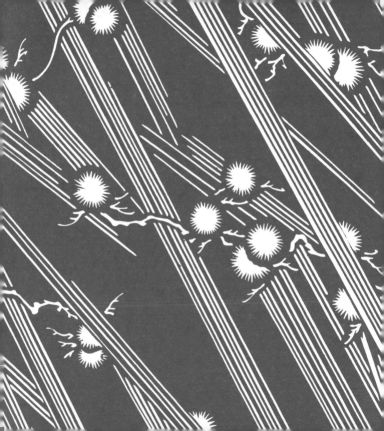

Go Out on
a Limb

Go out on a limb and see with what ease you can make one or two difficult decisions over the coming days.

The height of any person's accomplishments is usually directly proportionate to the depth of their convictions.

Suddenly you will find yourself wondering why you see mistakes less as something to lament and more as good ways of learning.
It is because you are confident.

Be confident in your friends and give them reason to have confidence in you.

Have confidence in truth, for there are only two mistakes one can make on the path to truth: not going all the way, and not starting at all.

Courage is not the absence of fear, but rather the confidence that something else is more important than fear.

Be confident that where there is love there is also woe. Better a life with woe than a life spent without knowing love.

It is best to act with confidence, no matter how little right you have to it.

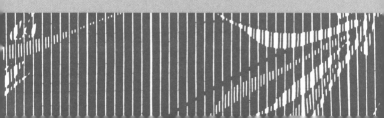

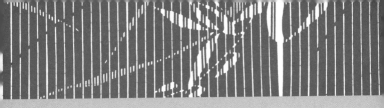

It is a person's own mind,
not some enemy or foe,
that leads a person to
evil ways.

Suddenly you will find yourself
wondering why all your indecision
has left you. It is because you
are confident.

Confident people accept luxuries into their lives only after their cost has been carefully considered.

Look for the people making all the excuses and you will locate the cause of most of the failures.

Anger will
never disappear
so long as
resentment is
in the mind.

A jug fills drop
by drop.
So it is with
confidence.

Your confidence can
dissolve all the anxiety
that surrounds your
responsibilities.

Confidence is perhaps the best gift we can possibly ever hope for after good health.

People whose minds have been shaped by selfless thoughts and acts give joy when they speak or act.

It is courageous to meet the facts of life face to face.

The first steps to developing confidence are not complex, but they demand questions, answers, and actions.

Confidence is a refreshing, clear, rejuvenating spring. When one chooses instead to drink from the Lake of Idleness, one instantly grows faint and weary.

No one deserves confidence who solicits it.

Avoid places that disturb your mind, and always remain where your virtues increase.

**Success
is the barrier of
distinction
that separates
confidence
and conceit.**

Do not look for
faults in others,
but look for faults in
yourself and purge
them like bad blood.

Where does danger breed best?
On a bed of too much confidence.

No person can claim to
hold power who has not
gained the people's
confidence.

No matter how
confident the lawyer,
the jury decides.

With confident optimism, all that exists becomes beautiful, or at least holds the potential for beauty.

There are three kinds of people: those who confidently roll up their sleeves and get stuck in, those who stick their noses in the air and turn away, and the others who just don't stick around at all.

Have confidence in those around you. Stop trying to tune them as separate instruments; inspire them as a whole and the result will be a symphony.

There is no pillow so soft as a clear conscience.

Look in the mirror and say aloud:
"I have always looked outside myself for strength and confidence, but it is within me right now, and has been there all this time."

Courage is a will so strong that it inspires us to want to succeed, no matter what the consequences.

Security is what we have when we know we can deal with the consequences that might arise.

Confidence comes from planning well, executing well, and, from having done something well, avoiding any negative consequences.

Without confidence, all belief becomes mere superstition.

A person gives a public speech that is five minutes long, and does it perfectly except for a minor stumble on a word halfway through. Would you focus on the four minutes and fifty-eight seconds that went well, or spend the rest of your day, week, year, or lifetime dwelling on the moment that went wrong?

There cannot be any success without self-confidence, and there can be no self-confidence without preparation.

Everybody grows and develops. It is knowing what you are growing toward that provides you with confidence in life.

Confident people examine
their plans before they act
—it is better than repenting
them afterward.

**It is human nature to
harbor doubt and feel
fear. These things never
leave us by our dwelling
on them: they must be
conquered through
finding the courage
to take action.**

Confidence is the first and finest of human qualities because it is the quality in a person which guarantees all others.

The best form of luck is to have been born a confident individual. With this gift, one always has at one's disposal the ability and determination to overcome bad luck.

There is no greater fool than a confident fool.

What is physical beauty without confidence?

To have to abandon anything can be a blow to anyone's self-confidence. It is learning how to look at what has been achieved and what may have been achieved under ideal circumstances, which can help us to regain confidence and go onward.

Life may demand us to be resolute or defiant, magnanimous or single-minded, but we should always have confidence in the potential for goodwill among mankind.

When you have learned to trust yourself, you will know how to live.

Have confidence in your strengths without boasting of them, and respect the strengths of others without fearing them.

Explore this world and explore your life in it, and if your journey brings you back to where you began, explore that place and get to know it for the very first time.

Confident people don't take life for granted. They have good days and great days, and look forward to better days to come.

Fear of discrimination and stigma can cause us, at any time, to lose faith in ourselves, resulting in social exclusion.

Natural confidence is not brash or loud: it is a quiet place.

Take pride in your own courage, whether it has been building a new career, beating addiction, or getting back into the world.

The confident mind sees a world
that is good and pleasant, inspiring,
and full of promise.

**No one can live your life
confidently except you.
You are responsible.**

Look in the mirror and say aloud:
"I am a likeable person."

One cannot cross the sea by standing at the water's edge.

Refuse to go through life being held back from what you want to do by fear.

Have the character and strength of will to say no when you should.

Those who wish to sing are always confident of finding the right song to suit their voice.

Where you were born and where you lived is of no importance. It is where you have been since, and what you have done in that time that people are interested in.

You need confidence to ask for what you are entitled to.

If you ask what the greatest accomplishment a person can make in a lifetime is, the answer would have to be the confidence to be themselves when everybody and everything is trying to make them into something else.

**Invest well in your appearance.
Let your look reflect the real you.**

Thinking honestly and deeply will help you to develop a whole new attitude toward the people you meet and the things that you do.

Live your life as calmly, patiently and trustfully as possible, but never allow yourself to be taken advantage of.

If you wish to display your confidence outwardly, act assertively, speak calmly, and always listen properly. Exhibit an aura of openness and fairness.

Skill and confidence together are unconquerable.

There is little point in starting along the road to confidence if you are not going to dedicate the time and effort necessary to get there.

We have to serve ourselves for many years before we gain our own confidence.

Confidence lives within all of us, waiting for us to take the first step to enter and search for it.

Your confidence can remove all fear of the future and replace it with enthusiasm and excitement.

To lead others confidently, one must first become convinced that a particular course of action is the right one, and then remain undaunted when the going gets tough.

You can expect with
confidence that accidents
will occur, but you can expect
with confidence to come
through them.

**It's easier to go down a hill than up it,
but the view is much better at the top.**

I am confident that there is a
solution for every difficulty
and that I can find it within me.

Are you embarrassed or humiliated about a certain aspect of your life? You can change your thinking to overcome this feeling— it's good to sometimes explore the flipside!

If you feel a lack of confidence, use the little you have to place yourself in a working or social environment with people who possess confidence, and be inspired by their examples.

Doubt your ability to accomplish something, and you probably won't accomplish it.

Confident people know that if their character is stable and orderly, their life will be too.

It takes great confidence to offer advice to those who think that they know everything already.

Let each today light your tomorrow.

A greedy heart is a heavier burden to bear than poverty, for it is never satisfied and always desires more.

Anything acquired through dishonesty leads to a severe loss of character.

Confident people do not need to rationalize greed in the name of doing good for causes that may make them appear respectable and praiseworthy.

Self-confidence removes all the unnecessary disturbance of envy and provides peace of mind.

Confident people are prepared to suffer for what they believe in and are usually forgiving of those who wrong them.

Confidence leads one to know and understand that there are certain limits in life.

Work harder at friendships—if you have none, acquire some through things that you are interested in.

Flirt more—it's an innocent pastime, most of us enjoy it, and it's a huge boost.

A confident person tends to be popular
and enjoyable to be around.
Their self-confidence is what makes
them attractive. It could be you.

Plot your route to achieving
everything you wish to achieve,
then set out to achieve it.

We all have rights and deserve to do only the things we want to.

Confident people don't allow their lives to be governed by "shoulds", "musts," and "ought-tos." If they had to have a motto, it would be "Why not?"

A journey to discovering confidence
is a journey to that rich inner place
where doubt does not exist.

**Confidence is a pact of trust and
certainty between you and yourself.**

You can measure a
person by what it takes
to discourage them.

You can be confident that criticism only grazes the skin and never wounds deeply.

What makes for a confident life? Everything hangs upon "if."

Each new thing we learn adds to our armor of confidence.

Confidence is a great equalizer. It can bring together people from obscure farms and the epicenter of metropolitan life.

Learn to love what is simple and beautiful in this life.

It takes great courage to be what we are. First we must escape from all false ties.

Have a little bit of confidence in life— it's the thing that holds all matter together.

Confidence is about understanding what sometimes blocks us from making decisions or taking certain actions, and knowing how and when to make a detour or plow on.

Confident people not only make successful business partners, but also life partners.

Never enter into a love life that you cannot bring your self-esteem to.

Pride in your sense of what is true for you is the path to confidence and inner peace.

Never settle for second best. It may seem easier at times, but it is not the real answer.

Make every day count as a good day. Add them all together and they will give you a great lifetime.

Who knows better than you how hard you work, how well you've done, and your successes. If you care for yourself, show it by giving praise where praise is due.

Everything can be taken from a person but one thing: their confidence in their ability to bounce back.

Just because some brute of a school bully told you that you were ugly twenty years ago, it doesn't mean that you are now. Let it go!

**Look confident.
Feeling good about yourself
on the outside will make you
feel great on the inside.**

Somebody is always doing
what somebody else said
couldn't be done.

**If every captain worried only about heavy
seas and the number of submerged rocks
out there, no ship would ever set sail.**

Confidence isn't gained by not falling, but from rising every time one does fall.

Educate yourself and the reward will be the ability to listen to criticism and advice objectively.

Men who have resolved to find a way for themselves will find opportunities.

An Hachette Livre UK Company

First published in Great Britain by MQ Publications
a division of Octopus Publishing Group Ltd
2–4 Heron Quays, London, E14 4JP
www.octopusbooks.co.uk

Copyright © Octopus Publishing Group Ltd 2007, 2008
Text © David Baird 2007

Distributed in the United States and Canada by
Hachette Book Group USA
237 Park Avenue
New York
NY 10017

All rights reserved. No part of this publication may used or
reproduced or transmitted in any form or by any means, electronic
or mechanical, including photocopying, recording, or any
information storage and retrieval system now known or to be
invented without permission in writing from the publishers.

David Baird asserts the moral right to be identified as the
author of this book.

ISBN 13: 978-1-84601-284-6
ISBN 10: 1-84601-284-8

A CIP catalogue record for this book is available from
the British Library.

10 9 8 7 6 5 4 3 2 1

Printed and bound in China